This book belongs to:

Santa Claus

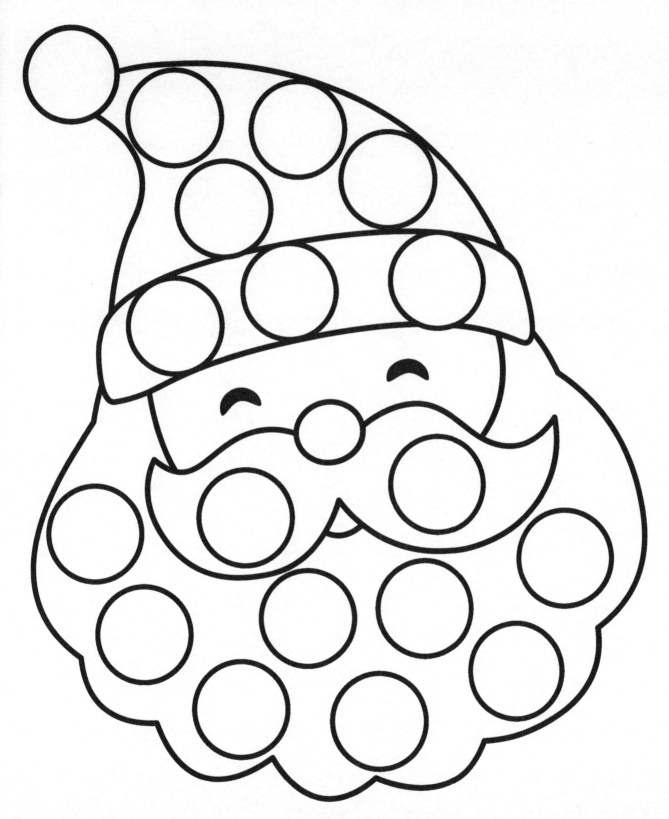

Reindeer

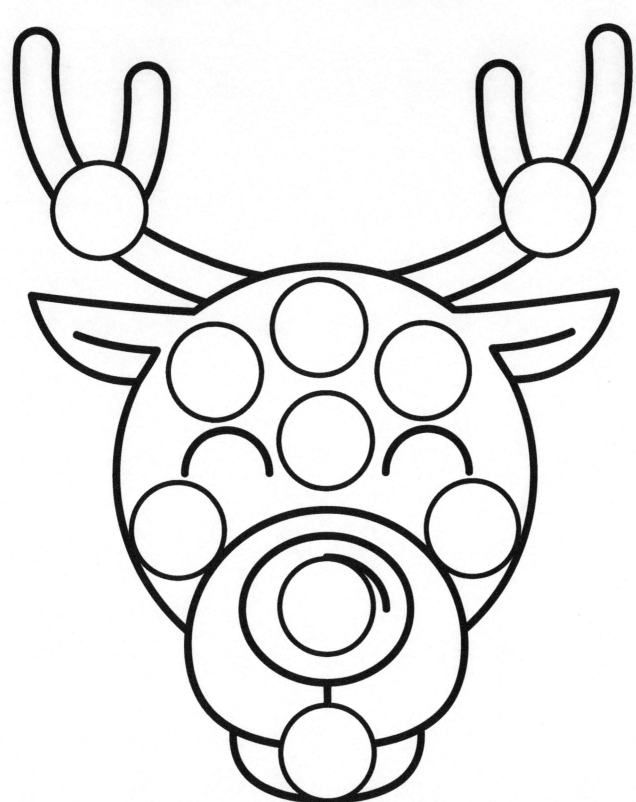

Reindeer

Christmas tree

Snowman

Candy cane

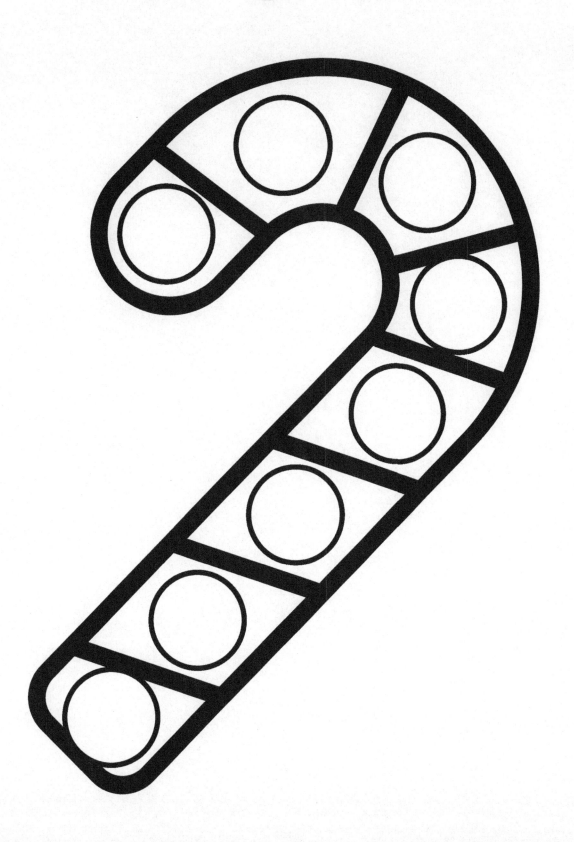

Elf

Christmas stocking

Christmas present

Christmas bell

Christmas
bell

Gingerbread
man

Wreath

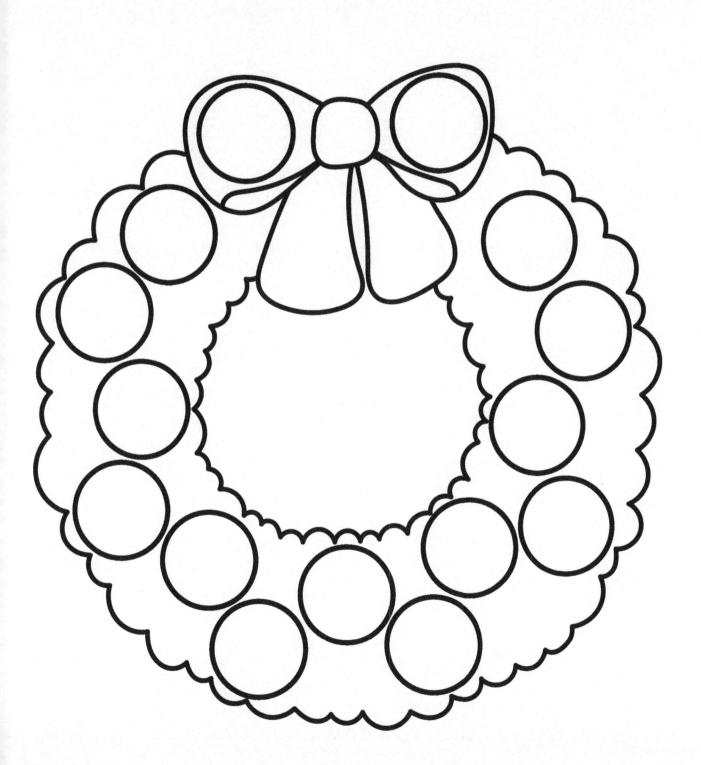

Wreath

Snowflake

Holly leaves and berries

Santa's sleigh

Santa's hat

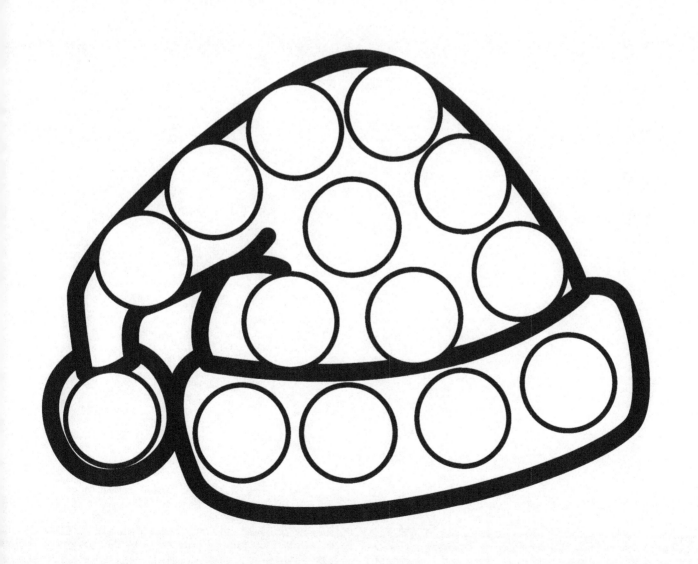

Christmas log

Christmas bauble

Polar bear

Fireplace with stockings

Angel

Toy train

Christmas star

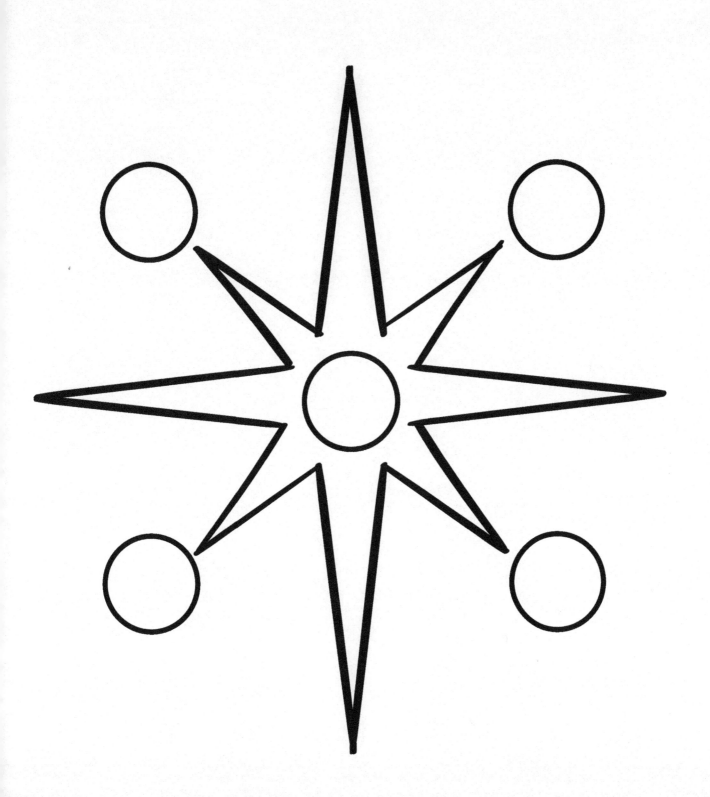

Christmas candle

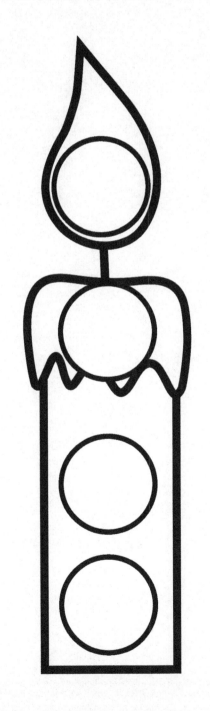

Penguin with scarf

Penguin with

scarf

Hot chocolate

Christmas mittens

Chimney with Santa

Ice skate

North Pole sign

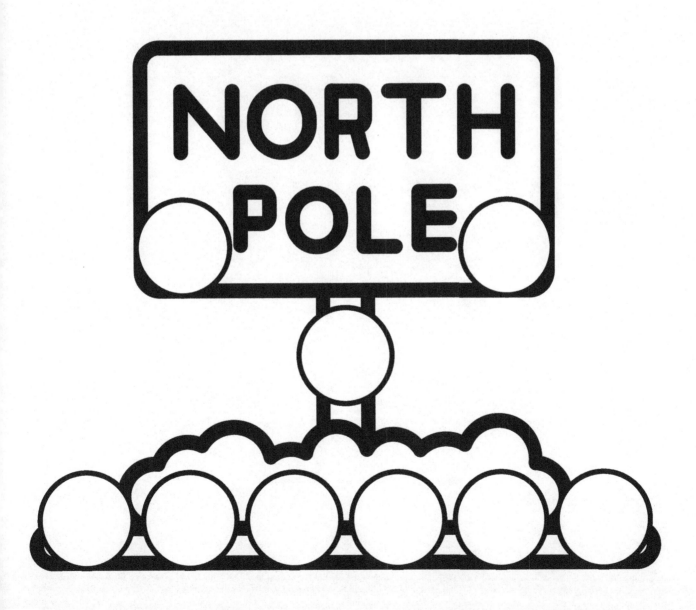

Santa's boots

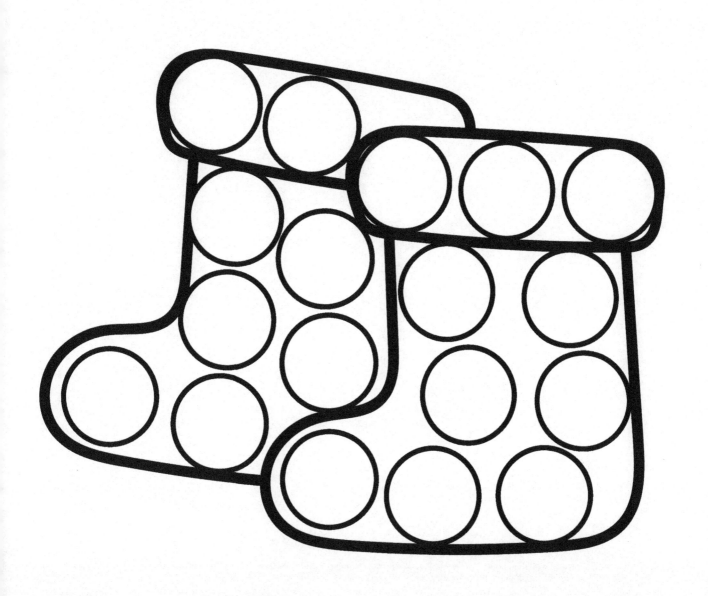

Christmas pudding

Christmas pudding

Festive garlands

Snowy clouds

Snowy clouds

Snow-covered mountains

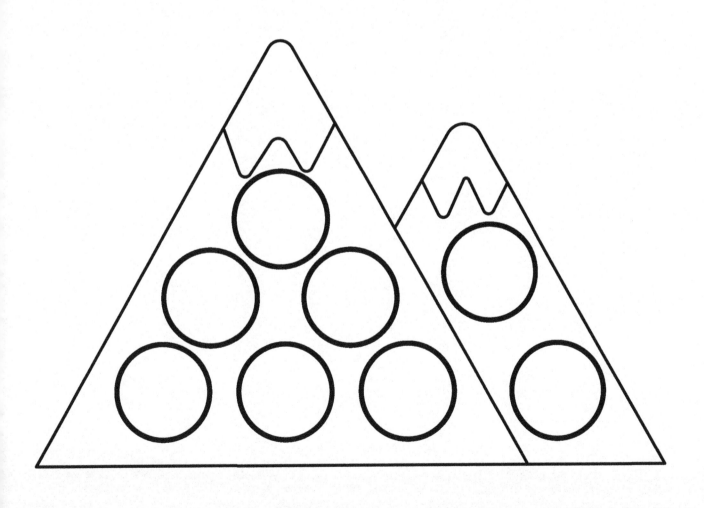

Beanie

Sled

Cozy scarf

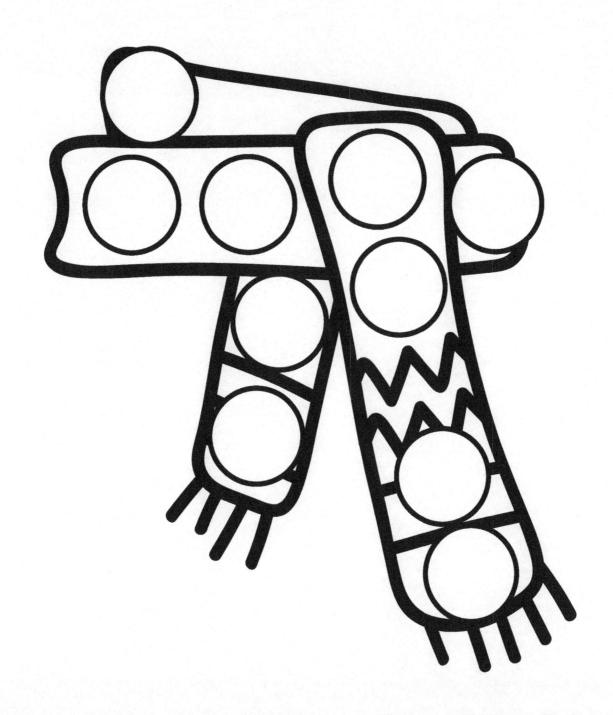

Christmas sweater

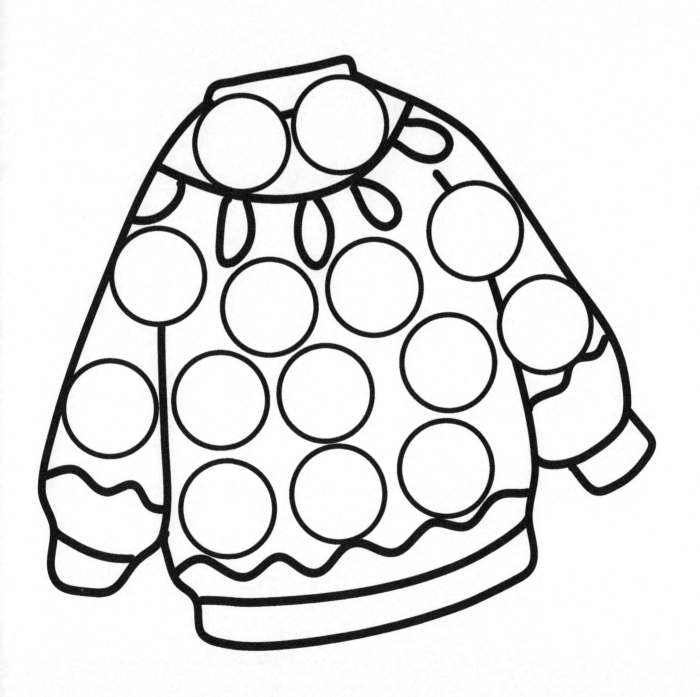

Winter house

Earmuffs

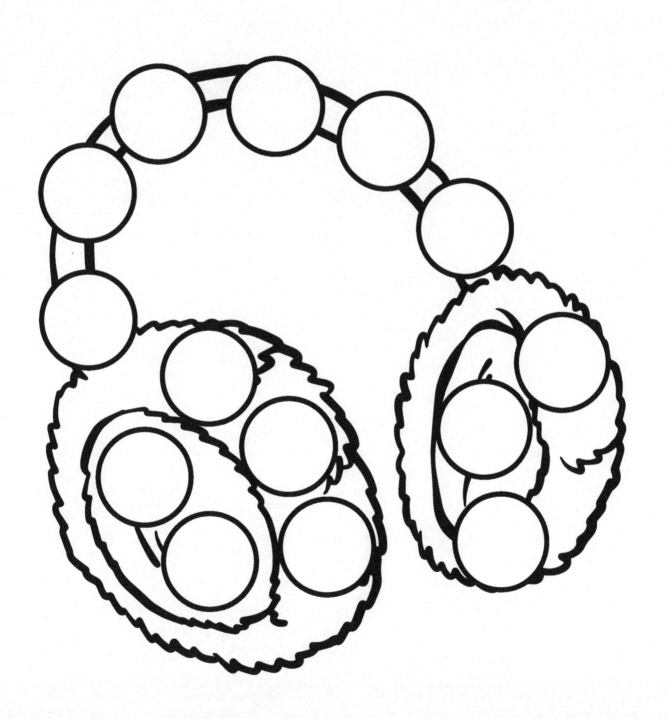

Snowball

Fireplace with flames

Snowmobile

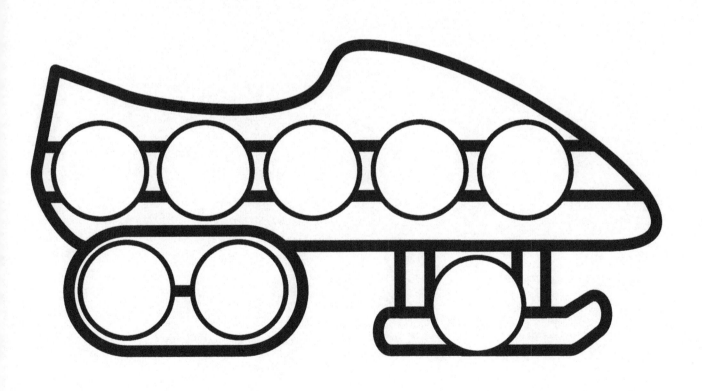

Pinecone

Teddy Bear

Christmas letter

Igloo

Igloo

Frost on windows

Sleigh bell

Made in United States
Orlando, FL
09 December 2024

55308195R00057